Prince2 Project Templates

PRINCE2™- BENEFITS MANAGEMENT APPROACH	4
PRINCE2™- BUSINESS CASE	7
PRINCE2™- CHECKPOINT REPORT	11
PRINCE2™- CHANGE CONTROL APPROACH	15
PRINCE2™- COMMUNICATION MANAGEMENT APPROACH	19
PRINCE2™- CONFIGURATION ITEM RECORD	24
PRINCE2™- CHANGE CONTROL APPROACH	27
PRINCE2™- DAILY LOG	31
PRINCE2™- END PROJECT REPORT	34
PRINCE2™- END STAGE REPORT	38
PRINCE2™- EXCEPTION REPORT	43
PRINCE2™- HIGHLIGHT REPORT	46
PRINCE2™- ISSUE REPORT	50
PRINCE2™- LESSONS REPORT	53
PRINCE2™- PLAN	57
PRINCE2™- PRODUCT DESCRIPTION	63
PRINCE2™- PRODUCT STATUS ACCOUNT	67
PRINCE2™- PROJECT BRIEF	70
PRINCE2™- PROJECT INITIATION DOCUMENTATION	74
PRINCE2™- PROJECT PRODUCT DESCRIPTION	80
PRINCE2™- QUALITY MANAGEMENT APPROACH	85
PRINCE2™- RISK MANAGEMENT APPROACH	89
PRINCE2™- WORK PACKAGE	94
CONCLUSION	100

Introduction

Project Management is an art form in itself and in order for it to be successful and applied well, it must be handled with care, with a focus upon details and a clear focus upon the end product.

The templates included can be amended to support any project, as with Prince2 being a methodology that can be used in any project or industry type, the purpose of this book and these templates is to support you and your organisation to be more successful when delivering projects

The core templates included can be downloaded when you send an email to the address at the end of the book.

The templates included are based upon the latest version of Prince2 2017 (the second updated from March 2017)

If you have recently completed the Prince2 Project Management training, these templates will enable you to start working immediately on projects and effectively help you manage the projects

PRINCE2™ - Benefits Management Approach

Project Name:			
Date:		**Release:**	Draft/Final
Author:			
Owner:			
Client:			
Document Number:			

Note: This document is only valid on the day it was printed

Revision History

Date of next revision:

Revision Date	Previous Revision Date	Summary of Changes	Changes Marked

Approvals

This document requires the following approvals. A signed copy should be placed in the project files.

Name	Signature	Title	Date of Issue	Version

Distribution

This document has been distributed to:

Name	Title	Date of Issue	Version

Overview

Purpose A Benefits Management Approach is used to define how and when a measurement of the achievement of the project's benefits, expected by the Senior User, can be made. The Plan is presented to the Executive during the Initiating a Project process, updated at each stage boundary, and used during the Closing a Project process to define any post-project benefits reviews that are required.

The plan has to cover the activities to find out whether the expected benefits of the products have been realized and how the products have performed when in operational use. Each expected benefit has to be assessed for the level of its achievement and whether any additional time is needed to assess the residual benefits. Use of the project's products may have brought unexpected side-effects, either beneficial or adverse. Time and effort have to be allowed to identify and analyse why these side effects were not foreseen.

If the project is part of a programme, the Benefits Management Approach may be contained within the programme's benefits realization plan and executed at the programme level. Post-project, the Benefits Management Approach is maintained and executed by corporate or programme management.

Contents The Benefits Management Approach should cover the following topics.

Benefit Matrix
The Project Product
Resourcing

Advice *The Benefits Management Approach is derived from the: Business Case, Project Product Description (in particular the acceptance Criteria) and if available the programme's benefits realization plan and the organisation's corporate performance monitoring function (e.g. centre of excellence).*

The Benefits Management Approach can take a number of formats, including: Document, spreadsheet or presentation slides; Entry in a project management tool.

The following quality criteria should be observed:
- *Covers all the benefits in the Business Case*
- *The benefits are measurable and baseline measures have been recorded*
- *Describes suitable timing for measurement of the benefits, together with reasons for the timing*
- *Identifies the skills or individuals who will be needed to carry out the measurements*
- *The effort and cost to undertake the benefits reviews is realistic when compared with the value of the anticipated benefits*
- *Consideration is given to whether dis-benefits should be measured and reviewed.*

Benefit Matrix

Ref no.	Benefit Description	Owner[1]	Measurement[2]		Resources[3]	Baseline[4]
			How	When		

The Project's Product
(In addition to the individual benefits of the project, provide some notes on how the performance of the overall Project's Product will be reviewed)

Resourcing
(Included against each benefit in the matrix but it may be helpful to provide some overall comments or requirements here)

---

[1] The Owner is the person who is accountable for the expected benefits
[2] Describe how to measure achievement of expected benefits, and when they can be measured
[3] What resources are needed to carry out the review work
[4] Baseline measures from which the improvements will be calculated

PRINCE2™ - Business Case

Project Name:			
Date:		**Release:**	Draft/Final
Author:			
Owner:			
Client:			
Document Number:			

Note: This document is only valid on the day it was printed

Revision History

Date of next revision:

Revision Date	Previous Revision Date	Summary of Changes	Changes Marked

Approvals

This document requires the following approvals. A signed copy should be placed in the project files.

Name	Signature	Title	Date of Issue	Version

Distribution

This document has been distributed to:

Name	Title	Date of Issue	Version

Overview

Purpose A Business Case is used to document the justification for the undertaking of a project, based on the estimated costs (of development, implementation and incremental ongoing operations and maintenance costs) against the anticipated benefits to be gained and offset by any associated risks.

The outline Business Case is developed in the Starting up a Project process and refined by the Initiating a Project process. The Directing a Project process covers the approval and re-affirmation of the Business Case.

The Business Case is used by the Controlling a Stage process when assessing impacts of issues and risks. It is reviewed and updated at the end of each management stage by the Managing a Stage Boundary process, and at the end of the project by the Closing a Project process.

Contents The Business Case should cover the following topics.

Executive Summary
Reasons
Business Options
Expected Benefits
Expected Dis-Benefits
Timescale
Costs
Investment Appraisal
Major Risks

Advice The Business Case is derived from the: Project mandate and Project Brief – reasons; Project Plan - costs and timescales; The Senior User(s) - expected benefits; The Executive - value for money; Risk Register and Issue Register.

The Business Case can take a number of formats, including: Document, spreadsheet or presentation slides; Entry in a project management tool.

The following quality criteria should be observed:
- The reasons for the project must be consistent with the corporate or programme strategy
- The Project Plan and Business Case must be aligned
- The benefits should be clearly identified and justified
- It should be clear how the benefits will be realized
- It should be clear what will define a successful outcome
- It should be clear what the preferred business option is, and why
- Where external procurement is required, it should be clear what the preferred sourcing option is, and why
- It should be clear how any necessary funding will be obtained
- The Business Case includes non-financial, as well as financial, criteria
- The Business Case includes operations and maintenance costs and risks, as well as project costs and risks
- The Business Case conforms to organizational accounting standards (e.g. break-even analysis and cash flow conventions)
- The major risks faced by the project are explicitly stated, together with any proposed responses.

Executive Summary
(Highlight the key points in the Business Case, which should include important benefits and the return on investment (ROI))

Reasons
(Defines the reasons for undertaking the project and explains how the project will enable the achievement of corporate strategies and objectives)

Business Options
(Analysis and reasoned recommendation for the base business options of: do nothing, do the minimal or do something)

Expected Benefits
(The benefits that the project will deliver expressed in measurable terms against the situation as it exists prior to the project. Benefits should be both qualitative and quantitative. They should be aligned to corporate or programme benefits. Tolerances should be set for each benefit and for the aggregated benefit. Any benefits realization requirements should be stated)

Expected Dis-benefits
(Outcomes perceived as negative by one or more stakeholders. Dis-benefits are actual consequences of an activity whereas, by definition, a risk has some uncertainty about whether it will materialize. For example, a decision to merge two elements of an organization onto a new site may have benefits (e.g. better joint working), costs (e.g. expanding one of the two sites) and dis-benefits (e.g. drop in productivity during the merger). Dis-benefits need to be valued and incorporated into the investment appraisal)

Timescale
(The period over which the project will run (summary of the Project Plan) and the period over which the benefits will be realized. This information is subsequently used to help timing decisions when planning (Project Plan, Stage Plan and Benefits Management Approach))

Costs
(A summary of the project costs (taken from the Project Plan), the ongoing operations and maintenance costs and their funding arrangements)

Investment Appraisal
(Compares the aggregated benefits and dis-benefits to the project costs (extracted from the Project Plan) and ongoing incremental operations and maintenance costs. The analysis may use techniques such as cash flow statement, ROI, net present value, internal rate of return and payback period. The objective is to be able to define the value of a project as an investment. The investment appraisal should address how the project will be funded)

Major Risks
(Gives a summary of the key risks associated with the project together with the likely impact and plans should they occur)

PRINCE2™ - Checkpoint Report

Project Name:			
Date:		**Release:**	Draft/Final
Author:			
Owner:			
Client:			
Document Number:			

Note: This document is only valid on the day it was printed

Revision History

Date of next revision:

Revision Date	Previous Revision Date	Summary of Changes	Changes Marked

Approvals

This document requires the following approvals. A signed copy should be placed in the project files.

Name	Signature	Title	Date of Issue	Version

Distribution

This document has been distributed to:

Name	Title	Date of Issue	Version

Overview

Purpose A Checkpoint Report is used to report, at a frequency defined in the Work Package, the status of the Work Package.

Contents The Checkpoint Report should cover the following topics.

> Follow ups from Previous Periods
> This Reporting Period
> Next Reporting Period
> Work Package Tolerance Status
> Issues & Risks

Advice The Checkpoint Report is derived from the: Work Packages; Team Plan and actuals and the previous Checkpoint Report

A Checkpoint Report can take a number of formats, including: Oral report to the Project Manager (could be in person or over the phone); Presentation at a review meeting (physical meeting or conference call); Document or email issued to the Project Manager; Entry in a project management tool.

The following quality criteria should be observed:

- Prepared at the frequency required by the Project Manager
- The level and frequency of progress assessment is right for the stage and/or Work Package
- The information is timely, useful, objective and accurate
- Every product in the Work Package, for that period, is covered by the report
- Includes an update on any unresolved issues from the previous report.

Date of Checkpoint	
Period Covered	

Follow ups from previous periods
(for example, action items completed or issues outstanding)

This Reporting Period

Products

Product Ref	Product name	Work undertaken	Date Completed

Quality Management
(activities undertaken this period

Lessons Identified

Next Reporting Period

Products

Product Ref	Product name	Work to be undertaken	Date to be Completed?

Quality Management
(activities planned for this period)

Work Package Tolerance Status
(How execution of the Work Package is performing against its tolerances (e.g. cost/time/scope actuals and forecast)

Issues and Risks
(Update on issues and risks associated with the Work Package)

PRINCE2™ - Change Control Approach

Project Name:			
Date:		**Release:**	Draft/Final
Author:			
Owner:			
Client:			
Document Number:			

Note: This document is only valid on the day it was printed

Revision History

Date of next revision:

Revision Date	Previous Revision Date	Summary of Changes	Changes Marked

Approvals

This document requires the following approvals. A signed copy should be placed in the project files.

Name	Signature	Title	Date of Issue	Version

Distribution

This document has been distributed to:

Name	Title	Date of Issue	Version

Overview

Purpose

A Change Control Approach is used to identify how, and by whom, the project's products will be controlled and protected. It answers the questions:

- How and where the project's products will be stored
- What storage and retrieval security will be put in place
- How the products and the various versions and variants of these will be identified
- How changes to products will be controlled
- Where responsibility for configuration management will lie.

Contents

The Change Control Approach should cover the following topics.

Introduction
Configuration Management Procedure
Issue & Change Control Procedure
Tools & Techniques
Records
Reporting
Timings of Configuration Management and Issue Control
Roles & Responsibilities
Scales for Priority & Severity

Advice

The Change Control Approach is derived from the: The customer's quality expectations; Corporate configuration management system (e.g. any configuration management software in use or mandated by the user); Programme Quality Management Strategy and information management strategy (if applicable); The user's quality management system; The supplier's quality management system; Specific needs of the project's product(s) and environment; Project management team structure (to identify those with configuration management responsibilities) and Facilitated workshops and informal discussions.

A Change Control Approach can take a number of formats, including: Stand-alone document or a section in the Project Initiation Document; Entry in a project management tool.

The following quality criteria should be observed:

- Responsibilities are clear and understood by both user and supplier
- The key identifier for the project's product(s) is defined
- The method and circumstances of version control are clear
- The strategy provides the Project Manager with all the product information required
- The corporate or programme strategy for configuration management has been considered
- The retrieval system will produce all required information in an accurate, timely and usable manner
- The project files provide the information necessary for any audit requirements
- The project files provide the historical records required to support any lessons
- The chosen Change Control Approach is appropriate for the size and nature of the project
- Resources are in place to administer the chosen method of configuration management
- The requirements of the operational group (or similar group to whom the project's product will be transitioned) should be considered.

Introduction
(States the purpose, objectives and scope, and identifies who is responsible for the strategy)

Configuration Management Procedure
(A description of (or reference to) the configuration management procedure to be used. Any variance from corporate or programme management standards should be highlighted, together with a justification for the variance. The procedure should cover activities such as planning, identification, control (including storage/retrieval, product
security, handover procedures etc.), status accounting, and verification and audit.)

Issue and Change Control Procedure
(A description (or reference to) the issue and change control procedures to be used. Any variance from corporate or programme management standards should be highlighted, together with a justification for the variance. The procedure should cover activities such as
capturing, examining, proposing, deciding and implementing.)

Tools and Techniques
(Refers to any configuration management systems or tools to be used and any preference for techniques that may be used for each step in the configuration management procedure)

Records
(Definition of the composition and format of the Issue Register and Configuration Item Records))

Reporting

(Describes the composition and format of the reports that are to be produced (Issue Report, Product Status Account), their purpose, timing and chosen recipients. This should include reviewing the performance of the procedures)

Timing of Configuration Management and Issue and Change Control Activities

(States when formal activities are to be undertaken, for example configuration audits)

Roles and Responsibilities

(Describes who will be responsible for what aspects of the procedures, including any corporate or programme management roles involved with the configuration management of the project's products. Describes whether a Change Authority and/or change budget will be established.)

Scales for Priority and Severity

(For prioritizing requests for change and off-specifications and for determining the level of management that can make decisions on severity of issue.)

PRINCE2™ - Communication Management Approach

Project Name:	
Date:	**Release:** Draft/Final
Author:	
Owner:	
Client:	
Document Number:	

Note: This document is only valid on the day it was printed

Revision History

Date of next revision:

Revision Date	Previous Revision Date	Summary of Changes	Changes Marked

Approvals

This document requires the following approvals. A signed copy should be placed in the project files.

Name	Signature	Title	Date of Issue	Version

Distribution

This document has been distributed to:

Name	Title	Date of Issue	Version

Overview

Purpose A Communication Management Approach contains a description of the means and frequency of communication to parties both internal and external to the project. It facilitates engagement with stakeholders through the establishment of a controlled and bi-directional flow of information.

Contents *The Communication Management Approach should cover the following topics.*

Introduction
Communication procedure
Tools & techniques
Records
Reporting
Timings of Communications Activities
Roles & Responsibilities
Stakeholder Analysis
Information Needs

Advice *The Communication Management Approach is derived from the:* Corporate communications policies (e.g. rules for disclosure for publicly listed companies); The programme's information Management Approach; Other components of the Project Initiation Documentation (in particular the project management team structure, the Risk Management Approach, Quality Management Approach and Configuration Management Strategy); Facilitated workshops/informal discussions with stakeholders; and Stakeholder analysis.

A Communication Management Approach can take a number of formats, including: Stand-alone product or a section in the Project Initiation Documentation; Document, spreadsheet or MindMap; Entry in a project management tool.

The following quality criteria should be observed:

- *All stakeholders have been identified and consulted for their communication requirements*
- *There is agreement from all stakeholders about the content, frequency and method of communication*
- *A common standard for communication has been considered*
- *The time, effort and resources required to carry out the identified communications have been allowed for in Stage Plans*
- *The formality and frequency of communication is reasonable for the project's importance and complexity*
- *For projects that are part of a programme, the lines of communication, and the reporting structure between the project and programme, have been made clear in the Communication Management Approach*
- *The Communication Management Approach incorporates corporate communications facilities where appropriate (e.g. using the marketing communications department for distributing project bulletins)*

Introduction
(States the purpose, objectives and scope, and identifies who is responsible for the strategy)

Communications Procedure
(A description of (or reference to) any communication methods to be used. Any variance from corporate or programme management standards should be highlighted, together with a justification for the variance)

Tools and Techniques
(Refers to any communication tools to be used, and any preference for techniques that may be used, for each step in the communication process)

Records
(Definition of what communication records will be required and where they will be stored (for example, logging of external correspondence))

Reporting
(Describes any reports on the communication process that are to be produced, including their purpose, timing and recipients (for example, performance indicators))

Timing of Communication Activities
(States when formal communication activities are to be undertaken (for example, at the end of a stage) including performance audits of the communication methods)

Roles and Responsibilities
(Describes who will be responsible for what aspects of the communication process, including any corporate or programme management roles involved with communication)

Stakeholder Analysis

Interested Party[5]	Current Relationship	Desired Relationship	Interfaces	Key Messages

---

[5] This may include accounts staff, user forum, internal audit, corporate or programme quality assurance, competitors etc.

Information Needs

Interested Party	Information for Distribution	Information for Collection	Information Provider and Recipient	Frequency of Communication	Means of Communication	Format of Communication

PRINCE2™ - Configuration Item Record

Project Name:			
Date:		**Release:** Draft/Final	
Author:			
Owner:			
Client:			
Document Number:			

Note: This document is only valid on the day it was printed

Revision History

Date of next revision:

Revision Date	Previous Revision Date	Summary of Changes	Changes Marked

Approvals

This document requires the following approvals. A signed copy should be placed in the project files.

Name	Signature	Title	Date of Issue	Version

Distribution

This document has been distributed to:

Name	Title	Date of Issue	Version

Overview

Purpose   To provide a record of such information as the history, status, version and variant of each configuration item, and any details of important relationships between them.

Contents   The Configuration Item Record should cover the following topics.

- Item Title
- Item Details

Advice   The Configuration Item Record is derived from the: Change Control Approach; Product breakdown structure; Stage Plan and Work Package; Quality Register, Issue Register and Risk Register.

The set of Configuration Item Records for a project is often referred to as a configuration library.

The Configuration Item Records can take a number of formats, including: Document, spreadsheet or database; Entry in a project management tool.

The following quality criteria should be observed:
- The records reflect the status of the products accurately
- The records are kept together in a secure location
- Version numbers match the actual products
- Configuration Item Records show products' version histories
- A process exists by which the Configuration Item Records are defined and updated.

Note: The following is a suggested list of components for each Configuration Item Record. The composition of a Configuration Item Record will be defined in the project's Change Control Approach so please check to see if the default list recommended here has been altered.

Unique Identifier

Project Identifier[6]	Item Identifier[7]	Current Version[8]

Note that when combined together these three uniquely identify the configuration item.

Item Title

(The description of the item (for a product this should be as it appears in the product breakdown structure))

Item Details

Date of last Status Change	
Owner[9]	
Location[10]	
Copy Holders[11]	
Item Type[12]	
Item Attributes[13]	
Stage[14]	
Users[15]	
Status[16]	
Product State[17]	
Variant[18]	
Producer[19]	
Date Allocated to the producer	
Source[20]	
Relationship with other items[21]	
Cross References[22]	

---

[6] Project Identifier – A unique reference. It will typically be a numeric or alpha-numeric value.
[7] Item Identifier – A unique reference. It will typically be a numeric or alpha-numeric value.
[8] Current Version – Typically an alpha-numeric value.
[9] The person or group who will take ownership of the product when it is handed over.
[10] Where the item is stored
[11] (if relevant), who currently has the product?
[12] Component, product, release (see section 9.2.2 of the manual)
[13] As defined by the Change Control Approach. These are used to specify a subset of products when producing a Product Status Account, such as the management stage in which the product is created, the type of product (e.g. hardware/ software), product destination etc.
[14] When the product will be developed
[15] The person or group who will use the item
[16] As defined by the Change Control Approach, e.g. pending development, in development, in review, approved or handed over
[17] (if used) As defined by the Product Description, e.g. dismantled machinery, moved machinery, reassembled machinery (see section 7.3.3.2 of the manual)
[18] (if used) for example, language variants
[19] The person or team responsible for creating or obtaining the item
[20] For example, in house, or purchased from a third-party company
[21] Those items that: Would be affected if this item changed; or if changed, would affect this item
[22] Issues and risks; or documentation that defines requirements, design, build, production and verification for the item (specifically this will include the Product Description)

PRINCE2™ - Change Control Approach

Project Name:	
Date:	**Release:** Draft/Final
Author:	
Owner:	
Client:	
Document Number:	

Note: This document is only valid on the day it was printed

Revision History

Date of next revision:

Revision Date	Previous Revision Date	Summary of Changes	Changes Marked

Approvals

This document requires the following approvals. A signed copy should be placed in the project files.

Name	Signature	Title	Date of Issue	Version

Distribution

This document has been distributed to:

Name	Title	Date of Issue	Version

Overview

Purpose A Change Control Approach is used to identify how, and by whom, the project's products will be controlled and protected. It answers the questions:

- How and where the project's products will be stored
- What storage and retrieval security will be put in place
- How the products and the various versions and variants of these will be identified
- How changes to products will be controlled
- Where responsibility for configuration management will lie.

Contents The Change Control Approach should cover the following topics.

Introduction
Change Control Procedure
Issue & Change Control Procedure
Tools & Techniques
Records
Reporting
Timings of Change Control Activities
Roles & Responsibilities
Scales of Priority & Severity

Advice The Change Control Approach is derived from the: The customer's quality expectations; Corporate configuration management system (e.g. any configuration management software in use or mandated by the user); Programme Quality Management Approach and information Management Approach (if applicable); The user's quality management system; The supplier's quality management system; Specific needs of the project's product(s) and environment; Project management team structure (to identify those with configuration management responsibilities) and Facilitated workshops and informal discussions.

A Change Control Approach can take a number of formats, including: Stand-alone document or a section in the Project Initiation Document; Entry in a project management tool.

The following quality criteria should be observed:

- Responsibilities are clear and understood by both user and supplier
- The key identifier for the project's product(s) is defined
- The method and circumstances of version control are clear
- The strategy provides the Project Manager with all the product information required
- The corporate or programme strategy for configuration management has been considered
- The retrieval system will produce all required information in an accurate, timely and usable manner
- The project files provide the information necessary for any audit requirements
- The project files provide the historical records required to support any lessons
- The chosen Change Control Approach is appropriate for the size and nature of the project
- Resources are in place to administer the chosen method of configuration management
- The requirements of the operational group (or similar group to whom the project's product will be transitioned) should be considered.

Introduction
(States the purpose, objectives and scope, and identifies who is responsible for the strategy)

Change Control Procedure
(A description of (or reference to) the configuration management procedure to be used. Any variance from corporate or programme management standards should be highlighted, together with a justification for the variance. The procedure should cover activities such as planning, identification, control (including storage/retrieval, product security, handover procedures etc.), status accounting, and verification and audit.)

Issue and Change Control Procedure
(A description (or reference to) the issue and change control procedures to be used. Any variance from corporate or programme management standards should be highlighted, together with a justification for the variance. The procedure should cover activities such as
capturing, examining, proposing, deciding and implementing.)

Tools and Techniques
(Refers to any configuration management systems or tools to be used and any preference for techniques that may be used for each step in the configuration management procedure)

Records
(Definition of the composition and format of the Issue Register and Configuration Item Records))

Reporting
(Describes the composition and format of the reports that are to be produced (Issue Report, Product Status Account), their purpose, timing and chosen recipients. This should include reviewing the performance of the procedures)

Timing of Issue and Change Control Activities
(States when formal activities are to be undertaken, for example configuration audits)

Roles and Responsibilities
(Describes who will be responsible for what aspects of the procedures, including any corporate or programme management roles involved with the configuration management of the project's products. Describes whether a Change Authority and/or change budget will be established.)

Scales for Priority and Severity
(For prioritizing requests for change and off-specifications and for determining the level of management that can make decisions on severity of issue.)

PRINCE2™ - Daily Log

Project Name:
Date: **Release:**   Draft/Final
Author:

Owner:

Client:

Document Number:

Note: This document is only valid on the day it was printed

Revision History
Date of next revision:

Revision Date	Previous Revision Date	Summary of Changes	Changes Marked

Approvals

This document requires the following approvals. A signed copy should be placed in the project files.

Name	Signature	Title	Date of Issue	Version

Distribution

This document has been distributed to:

Name	Title	Date of Issue	Version

Overview

Purpose A Daily Log is used to record informal issues, required actions or significant events not caught by other PRINCE2 registers or logs. It acts as the project diary for the Project Manager.

It can also be used as a repository for issues and risks during the Starting up a Project process if the other registers have not been set up.

There may be more than one Daily Log as Team Managers may elect to have one for their Work Packages, separate from the Project Manager's Daily Log.

Contents *The Daily Log is in free form but it is likely to include date, event, responsibility and result information as proposed in the following grid.*

Advice *Entries are made when the Project Manager or Team Manager feels it is appropriate to log some event. Often entries are based on thoughts, conversations and observations.*

A Daily Log can take a number of formats including a Document or Spreadsheet; Desk diary or log book; Electronic diary/calendar/task lists or Entry in a project management tool.

The following quality criteria should be observed:

- *Entries are sufficiently documented to be understandable later (a short note might make sense at the time, but will it in several months' time?)*
- *Date, person responsible and target date are always filled in*
- *Consideration has been given to access rights for the Daily Log (e.g. should the Daily Log be visible to everyone working on the project?).*

Log Contents

Date of Entry	Problem, Action, Event or Comment	Person Responsible	Target Date	Results

PRINCE2™ - End Project Report

Project Name:	
Date:	**Release:** Draft/Final
Author:	
Owner:	
Client:	
Document Number:	

Note: This document is only valid on the day it was printed

Revision History

Date of next revision:

Revision Date	Previous Revision Date	Summary of Changes	Changes Marked

Approvals

This document requires the following approvals. A signed copy should be placed in the project files.

Name	Signature	Title	Date of Issue	Version

Distribution

This document has been distributed to:

Name	Title	Date of Issue	Version

Overview

Purpose An End Project Report is used during project closure to review how the project performed against the version of the Project Initiation Documentation used to authorize it. It also allows the:

- Passing on of any lessons that can be usefully applied to other projects
- Passing on of details of unfinished work, ongoing risks or potential product modifications to the group charged with future support of the project's products in their operational life.

Contents The End Project Report should cover the following topics.

Project Managers Report
Review of the Business Case
Review of Project Activities
Review of Team Performance
Lessons Report
Review of Products

Advice The End Project Report is derived from the: Project Initiation Documentation; Business Case; Project Plan; Benefits Management Approach; Issue Register, Quality Register and Risk Register; Lessons Report and End Stage Reports (and Exceptions Reports, if applicable).

An End Project Report can take a number of formats, including presentation to the Project Board (physical meeting or conference call), as a document or email issued to the Project Board or as an entry in a project management tool.

The following quality criteria should be observed:

- Any abnormal situations are described, together with their impact
- At the end of the project, all issues should either be closed or become the subject of a follow-on action recommendation
- Any available useful documentation or evidence should accompany the follow-on action recommendation(s)
- Any appointed Project Assurance roles should agree with the report.

Project Manager's report
(Summarizing the project's performance)

Review of the Business Case
(Summarizing the validity of the project's Business Case)

Benefits achieved to date

Residual benefits expected
(post-project)

Expected net benefits

Deviations from the approved Business Case

Review of Project Objectives
(Review of how the project performed against its planned targets and tolerances for time, cost, quality, scope, benefits and risk. Review the effectiveness of the project's strategies and controls)

Review of Team Performance
(In particular, providing recognition for good performance)

Lessons Report
(A review of what went well, what went badly, and any recommendations for corporate or programme management consideration (and if the project was prematurely closed, then the reasons should be explained). This may be a separate document and referenced from this location

Review of Products

Product Name	Quality Records[23]		Approval Records[24]	Off-specifications[25]
	Planned	Completed		

Project Product Handover

(Confirmation (in the form of acceptance records) by the customer that operations and maintenance functions are ready to receive the project's product)

Summary of Follow-on Action Recommendations

(Request for Project Board advice about who should receive each recommended action. The recommended actions are related to unfinished work, ongoing issues and risks, and any other activities needed to take the products to the next phase of their life)

---

[23] Quality activities planned and completed
[24] The Requisite approvals for each Product
[25] Any missing products or products which do not meet the original requirements, and confirmation of any concessions granted

PRINCE2™ - End Stage Report

Project Name:			
Date:		**Release:**	Draft/Final
Author:			
Owner:			
Client:			
Document Number:			

Note: This document is only valid on the day it was printed

Revision History

Date of next revision:

Revision Date	Previous Revision Date	Summary of Changes	Changes Marked

Approvals

This document requires the following approvals. A signed copy should be placed in the project files.

Name	Signature	Title	Date of Issue	Version

Distribution

This document has been distributed to:

Name	Title	Date of Issue	Version

Overview

Purpose An End Stage Report is used to give a summary of progress to date, the overall project situation, and sufficient information to ask for a Project Board decision on what to do next with the project.

The Project Board uses the information in the End Stage Report in tandem with the next Stage Plan to decide what action to take with the project: for example, authorize the next stage, amend the project scope, or stop the project.

Contents *The End Stage Report should cover the following topics.*

Project Managers Report
Review of the Business Case
Review of Project Objectives
Review of Stage Objectives
Review of Team Performance
Lessons Report
Issues & Risks
Forecast
Review of Products

Note: Where the End Stage Report is being produced at the end of the initiation stage, not all of the above content may be appropriate or necessary.

Advice *The End Stage Report is derived from the: Current Stage Plan and actuals; Project Plan; Benefits Management Approach; Issue Register, Quality Register and Risk Register; Exception Report (if applicable); Lessons Report; Completed/slipped Work Packages and updated Business Case.*

An End Stage Report can take a number of formats, including presentation to the Project Board (physical meeting or conference call), as a document or email issued to the Project Board; or as an entry in a project management tool.

The following quality criteria should be observed:
- The report clearly shows stage performance against the plan
- Any abnormal situations are described, together with their impact
- Any appointed Project Assurance roles agree with the report.

Project Manager's Report
(Summarizing the stage performance)

Review of the Business Case
(Summarizing the validity of the project's Business Case)

Benefits achieved to date

Residual benefits expected
(remaining stages and post-project)

Expected net benefits

Deviations from the approved Business Case

Aggregated risk exposure

Review of Project Objectives
(Review of how the project has performed to date against its planned targets and tolerances for time, cost, quality, scope, benefits and risk. Review the effectiveness of the project's strategies and controls)

Review of Stage Objectives
(Review of how the specific stage performed against its planned targets and tolerances for time, cost, quality, scope, benefits and risk)

Review of Team Performance
(In particular, providing recognition for good performance)

Lessons Report
(A review of what went well, what went badly, and any recommendations for corporate or programme management consideration)

Issues and Risks
(Summary of the current set of issues and risks affecting the project)

Forecast
(The Project Manager's forecast for the project and next stage against planned targets and tolerances for time, cost, quality, scope, benefits and risk)

Review of Products

Product Name	Quality Records[26]		Approval Records[27]	Off-specifications[28]
	Planned	Completed		

---

[26] Quality activities planned and completed in the stage
[27] The Requisite approvals for each Product planned for completion in the stage
[28] Any missing products or products which do not meet the original requirements, and confirmation of any concessions granted

Phased Handover (if applicable)

(Confirmation by the customer that operations and maintenance functions are ready to receive the release)

Summary of Follow-on Action Recommendations (if applicable)

(Request for Project Board advice about who should receive each recommended action. The recommended actions are related to unfinished work, ongoing issues and risks, and any other activities needed to take the products handed over to the next phase of their life)

PRINCE2™ - Exception Report

Project Name:			
Date:		Release:	Draft/Final
Author:			
Owner:			
Client:			
Document Number:			

Note: This document is only valid on the day it was printed

Revision History

Date of next revision:

Revision Date	Previous Revision Date	Summary of Changes	Changes Marked

Approvals

This document requires the following approvals. A signed copy should be placed in the project files.

Name	Signature	Title	Date of Issue	Version

Distribution

This document has been distributed to:

Name	Title	Date of Issue	Version

Overview

Purpose An Exception Report is produced when a Stage Plan or Project Plan is forecast to exceed tolerance levels set. It is prepared by the Project Manager in order to inform the Project Board of the situation, and to offer options and recommendations for the way to proceed.

Contents The Exception Report should cover the following topics.

Title
Cause
Consequences
Options
Recommendation
Lessons

Advice *The Exception Report is derived from the: Current plan and actuals; Issue Register, Risk Register and Quality Register; Highlight Reports (for stage/project-level deviations) or Checkpoint Reports (for team-level deviations) and Project Board advice of an external event that affects the project.*

An Exception Report can take a number of formats, including as an Issue raised at a minuted progress review (physical meeting or conference call), as a document or email issued to the next-higher level of management or as an entry in a Project Management Tool. For urgent exceptions, it is recommended that the Exception Report is oral in the first instance, and then followed-up in the agreed format.

The following quality criteria should be observed:

- The current plan must accurately show the status of time and cost performance
- The reason(s) for the deviation must be stated, the exception clearly analysed, and any impacts assessed and fully described
- Implications for the Business Case have been considered and the impact on the overall Project Plan has been calculated
- Options are analysed (including any risks associated with them) and recommendations are made for the most appropriate way to proceed
- The Exception Report is given in a timely and appropriate manner.

Title
(An overview of the exception being reported)

Cause
(A description of the cause of a deviation from the current plan)

Consequences
(What the implications are if the deviation is not addressed for; The project; Corporate or Programme Management)

Options
(What are the options that are available to address the deviation and what would the effect of each option be on the Business Case, risks and tolerances)

Recommendation
(Of the available options, what is the recommendation, and why?)

Lessons
(What can be learned from the exception, on this project or future projects)

PRINCE2™ - Highlight Report

Project Name:			
Date:		**Release:**	Draft/Final
Author:			
Owner:			
Client:			
Document Number:			

Note: This document is only valid on the day it was printed

Revision History
Date of next revision:

Revision Date	Previous Revision Date	Summary of Changes	Changes Marked

Approvals

This document requires the following approvals. A signed copy should be placed in the project files.

Name	Signature	Title	Date of Issue	Version

Distribution

This document has been distributed to:

Name	Title	Date of Issue	Version

Overview

Purpose A Highlight Report is used to provide the Project Board (and possibly other stakeholders) with a summary of the stage status at intervals defined by them. The Project Board uses the report to monitor stage and project progress. The Project Manager also uses it to advise the Project Board of any potential problems or areas where the Project Board could help.

Contents The Highlight Report should cover the following topics.

> Status Summary
> This Reporting Period
> Next Reporting Period
> Project & Stage Tolerance Status
> Requests for Change
> Key Issues & Risks
> Lessons Report (If appropriate)

Advice The Highlight Report is derived from the: Project Initiation Documentation; Checkpoint Reports; Issue Register, Quality Register and Risk Register; Stage Plan and actuals: and Communication Management Approach

The Highlight Report can take a number of formats, including: Presentation to the Project Board (physical meeting or conference call); Document or email to the Project Board; Entry in a project management tool.

The following quality criteria should be observed:
- The level and frequency of progress reporting required by the Project Board is right for the stage and/or project
- The Project Manager provides the Highlight Report at the frequency, and with the content, required by the Project Board
- The information is timely, useful, accurate and objective
- The report highlights any potential problem areas.

Date of Highlight Report	
Period Covered	

Status Summary
(An overview of the status of the stage at this time)

This Reporting Period

Work Packages

Work Package Ref	Work Package Name	Status[29]	Notes[30]

Products

Product Ref	Product name	Status[31]	Notes[32]

Corrective Actions Undertaken
(Taken during the period)

---

[29] Either Pending Authorisation, In Execution or Completed (in the period)
[30] For example, if Work Packages are being performed by external suppliers, this information may be accompanied by purchase order and invoicing data
[31] Completed (in the period), Planned (but not started or completed) or Underway (as planned)
[32] Indicate if any products are running behind schedule.

Next Reporting Period

Work Packages

Work Package Ref	Work Package Name	Status[33]	Notes[34]

Products to be completed

Product Ref	Product name	Notes

Corrective Actions
(To be completed during the next period)

Project and Stage Tolerance Status
(How execution of the project and stage are performing against its tolerances (e.g. cost/time/scope actuals and forecast))

Requests for Change
(Identifying any raised, approved/rejected and pending)

Key Issues and Risks
(Summary of actual or potential problems and risks)

Lessons Report (if appropriate)
(A review of what went well, what went badly, and any recommendations for corporate or programme

---

[33] Either To be authorized, In-execution, and To be completed during the next period
[34] For example, if Work Packages are being performed by external suppliers, this information may be accompanied by purchase order and invoicing data

management consideration)

PRINCE2™ - Issue Report

Project Name:			
Date:		**Release:** Draft/Final	
Author:			
Owner:			
Client:			
Document Number:			

Note: This document is only valid on the day it was printed

Revision History
Date of next revision:

Revision Date	Previous Revision Date	Summary of Changes	Changes Marked

Approvals

This document requires the following approvals. A signed copy should be placed in the project files.

Name	Signature	Title	Date of Issue	Version

Distribution

This document has been distributed to:

Name	Title	Date of Issue	Version

Overview

Purpose An Issue Report is a report containing the description, impact assessment and recommendations for a request for change, off-specification or a problem/concern. It is only created for those issues that need to be handled formally.

The report is initially created when capturing the issue and updated both after the issue has been examined and when proposals are identified for issue resolution. The Issue Report is later amended further in order to record what option was decided upon, and finally updated when the implementation has been verified and the issue is closed.

Contents The Issue Report should cover the following topics.

Issue Report

Note: this is a default template format, please check with the Change Control Approach for precise format and composition requirements

Advice The Issue Report is derived from the: Highlight Report(s), Checkpoint Report(s) and End Stage Report(s); Stage Plan together with actual values and events; Users and supplier teams working on the project; The application of quality controls; Observation and experience of the processes; Quality Register, Risk Register and Lessons Log; and Completed Work Packages.

The Issue Report can take a number of formats, including: Document, spreadsheet or database; Entry in a project management tool.

Not all entries in the Issue Register will need a separately documented Issue Report.

The following quality criteria should be observed:
- The issue stated is clear and unambiguous
- A detailed impact analysis has occurred
- All implications have been considered
- The issue has been examined for its effect on the tolerances
- The issue has been correctly registered on the Issue Register
- Decisions are accurately and unambiguously described.

Issue Report

Issue ID[35]		Issue Type[36]	
Date Raised		Raised by[37]	
Issue Report Author[38]			
Issue Description[39]			
Impact Analysis[40]			
Recommendation[41]			
Priority[42]			
Severity[43]			
Decision[44]			
Decision Date		Approved By[45]	
Closure Date[46]			

---

[35] As shown in the Issue Register (provides the unique reference for every Issue Report)
[36] Defines the type of Issue being recorded, namely: request for change; off-specification or problem/concern
[37] The name of the individual or team who raised the issue
[38] The name of the individual or team who created the Issue Report
[39] A statement describing the issue in terms of its cause and impact
[40] A detailed analysis of the likely impact of the issue. This may include, for example, a list of products impacted.
[41] A description of what the Project Manager believes should be done to resolve the issue (and why)
[42] This should be given in terms of the project's chosen scale. It should be re-evaluated after impact analysis
[43] This should be given in terms of the project's chosen scale. Severity will indicate what level of management is required to make a decision on the issue.
[44] The decision made: Accept, Reject, Defer or Grant Concession)
[45] A record of who made the decision
[46] The date that the issue was closed

PRINCE2™ - Lessons Report

Project Name:			
Date:		**Release:**	Draft/Final
Author:			
Owner:			
Client:			
Document Number:			

Note: This document is only valid on the day it was printed

Revision History

Date of next revision:

Revision Date	Previous Revision Date	Summary of Changes	Changes Marked

Approvals

This document requires the following approvals. A signed copy should be placed in the project files.

Name	Signature	Title	Date of Issue	Version

Distribution

This document has been distributed to:

Name	Title	Date of Issue	Version

Lessons Report <Insert Project Name> Created/updated 04/04/18

Overview

Purpose The Lessons Report is used to pass on any lessons that can be usefully applied to other projects. The purpose of the report is to provoke action so that the positive lessons become embedded in the organization's way of working, and that the organization is able to avoid any negative lessons on future projects.

A Lessons Report can be created at any time in a project and should not necessarily wait to the end. Typically, it should be included as part of the End Stage Report and End Project Report. It may be appropriate (and necessary) for there to be several Lessons Reports specific to the particular organization (e.g. user, supplier, corporate or programme).

The data in the report should be used by the corporate group that is responsible for the quality management system, in order to refine, change and improve the standards. Statistics on how much effort was needed for products can help improve future estimating.

Contents The Lessons Report should cover the following topics.

Executive Summary
Overall Review
Review of Useful Measures
Significant Lessons

Advice *The Lessons Report is derived from the following documents:* Project Initiation Documentation (for the baseline position); Lessons Log (for identification of lessons); Quality Register, Issue Register and Risk Register (for statistical analysis); Quality records (for statistical analysis) and Communication Management Approach (for the distribution list).

The Lessons Report can take a number of formats, including: Oral report to the Project Board (could be in person or over the phone); Presentation at a progress meeting (physical meeting or conference call); Document or email to the Project Board; Entry in a project management tool.

The following quality criteria should be observed:
- Every management control has been examined
- Statistics of estimates versus actuals are *provided*
- Statistics of the success of quality controls used are included
- Any appointed Project Assurance roles agree with the report
- Unexpected risks are reviewed to determine whether they could have been anticipated
- Recommended actions are provided for each lesson (note that lessons are not 'learned' until action is taken).

Lessons Report <Insert Project Name> Created/updated 04/04/18

Executive Summary
(Specify the scope of the report e.g. Stage or Project)

Overall Review
(A review of what went well, what went badly and any recommendations for corporate or programme management consideration. In particular: Project management method (including the tailoring of PRINCE2); Any specialist methods used; Project strategies (risk management, quality management, communications management and configuration management); Project controls (and the effectiveness of any tailoring) and Abnormal events causing deviations)

Review of Useful Measures
(Such as: How much effort was required to create the products; How effective was the Quality Management Approach in designing, developing and delivering fit-for-purpose products (for example, how many errors were found after products had passed quality inspections?) and Statistics on issues and risks)

Significant Lessons

For Significant lessons it may be useful to provide additional details as follows.

Event	Effect[47]	Causes/Trigger	Early Warnings?[48]	Identified as a Risk?[49]	Recommendations

---

[47] For example, caused a positive/negative financial impact
[48] Where there any early-warning indicators?
[49] Was the triggered event previously identified as a risk (threat or opportunity)?

PRINCE2™- Plan

Project Name:	
Date:	**Release:** Draft/Final
Author:	
Owner:	
Client:	
Document Number:	

Note: This document is only valid on the day it was printed

Revision History

Date of next revision:

Revision Date	Previous Revision Date	Summary of Changes	Changes Marked

Approvals

This document requires the following approvals. A signed copy should be placed in the project files.

Name	Signature	Title	Date of Issue	Version

Distribution

This document has been distributed to:

Name	Title	Date of Issue	Version

Overview

Purpose

A plan provides a statement of how and when objectives are to be achieved, by showing the major products, activities and resources required for the scope of the plan. In PRINCE2, there are three levels of plan: project, stage and team. Team Plans are optional and may not need to follow the same composition as a Project Plan or Stage Plan.

An Exception Plan is created at the same level as the plan that it is replacing.

A Project Plan provides the Business Case with planned costs, and it identifies the management stages and other major control points. It is used by the Project Board as a baseline against which to monitor project progress.

Stage Plans cover the products, resources, activities and controls specific to the stage and are used as a baseline against which to monitor stage progress.

Team Plans (if used) could comprise just a schedule appended to the Work Package(s) assigned to the Team Manager.

A plan should cover not just the activities to create products but also the activities to manage product creation - including activities for assurance, quality management, risk management, configuration management, communication and any other project controls required.

Contents

The Plan should cover the following topics.
- Plan Description   4
- Plan Prerequisites   4
- External Dependencies   4
- Planning Assumptions   4
- Lessons Incorporated   5
- Monitoring and Control   5
- Budgets   5
- Tolerances   5
- Product Descriptions   5
- Schedule   6

Advice

The Plan is derived from the Project Brief, Quality Management Approach (for quality management activities to be included in the plan), Risk Management Approach (for risk management activities to be included in the plan), Communication Management Approach (for communication management activities to be included in the plan), Change Control Approach (for configuration management activities to be included in the plan), Resource availability, and Registers and logs.

The Plan can take a number of formats including: A stand-alone document or a section of the Project Initiation Documentation; Document, spreadsheet, presentation slides or MindMap; Entry in a project management tool.

The schedule may be in the form of a product checklist (which is a list of the products to be delivered within the scope of the plan, together with key status dates such as draft ready, quality inspected, approved etc.) or the output from a project planning tool.

The following quality criteria should be observed:
- The plan is achievable

- Estimates are based on consultation with the resources, who will undertake the work, and/or historical data
- Team Managers agree that their part of the plan is achievable
- It is planned to an appropriate level of detail (not too much, not too little)
- The plan conforms to required corporate or programme standards
- The plan incorporates lessons from previous projects
- The plan incorporates any legal requirements
- The Plan covers management and control activities (such as quality) as well as the activities to create the products in scope
- **The plan supports the Quality Management Approach, Change Control Approach**, Risk Management Approach, Communication Management Approach and project approach
- The plan supports the management controls defined in the Project Initiation Documentation

Plan Description
(Covering a brief description of what the plan encompasses (i.e. project, stage, team, exception) and the planning approach)

Plan Prerequisites
(Containing any fundamental aspects that must be in place, and remain in place, for the plan to succeed)

External Dependencies
(That may influence the plan)

Planning Assumptions
(Upon which the plan is based)

Lessons Incorporated
(Details of relevant lessons from previous similar projects, which have been reviewed and accommodated within this plan)

Monitoring and Control
(Details of how the plan will be monitored and controlled)

Budgets
(Covering time and cost, including provisions for risks and changes)

Tolerances
(Time, cost and scope tolerances for the level of plan (which may also include more specific stage- or team-level risk tolerances))

Product Descriptions
(Covering the products within the scope of the plan (for the Project Plan this will include the project's product; for the Stage Plan this will be the stage products; and for a Team Plan this should be a reference to the Work Package assigned). Quality tolerances will be defined in each Product Description)

Schedule
This may include or reference graphical representations of the following:
- Gantt or bar chart
- Product breakdown structure
- Product flow diagram
- Activity Network
- Table of resource requirements – by resource type (e.g. four engineers, one test manager, one business analyst)
- Table of requested/assigned specific resources – by name (e.g. Nikki, Jay, Francesca)

The Schedule may also be in the form of a Product Checklist as shown below

Product Identifier	Product Title	Product Description approved		Draft Ready		Final Quality Check completed		Approved		Handed Over (if applicable)	
		Plan	Actual	Plan	Actual	Plan	Actual	Plan	Actual	Plan	Actual

PRINCE2™ - Product Description

Project Name:	
Date:	**Release:** Draft/Final
Author:	
Owner:	
Client:	
Document Number:	

Note: This document is only valid on the day it was printed

Revision History

Date of next revision:

Revision Date	Previous Revision Date	Summary of Changes	Changes Marked

Approvals

This document requires the following approvals. A signed copy should be placed in the project files.

Name	Signature	Title	Date of Issue	Version

Distribution

This document has been distributed to:

Name	Title	Date of Issue	Version

Overview

Purpose A Product Description is used to:

- Understand the detailed nature, purpose, function and appearance of the product
- Define who will use the product
- Identify the sources of information or supply for the product
- Identify the level of quality required of the product
- Enable identification of activities to produce, review and approve the product
- Define the people or skills required to produce, review and approve the product.

Contents A Product Description should cover the following topics.

Purpose
Composition
Derivation
Format & Presentation
Development Skills Required
Quality Criteria
Quality Tolerance
Quality Method
Quality Skills Required
Quality Responsibilities

Advice *A product Description is derived from the Product breakdown structure, The end-users of the product, Quality Management Approach and the Change Control Approach.*

A Product Description can take a number of formats, including: Document, presentation slides or mind map; Entry in a project management tool.

The following quality criteria should be observed:

- The purpose of the product is clear and is consistent with other products
- The product is described to a level of detail sufficient to plan and manage its development
- The Product Description is concise yet sufficient to enable the product to be produced, reviewed and approved
- Responsibility for the development of the product is clearly identified
- Responsibility for the development of the product is consistent with the roles and responsibilities described in the project management team organization and the Quality Management Approach
- The quality criteria are consistent with the project quality standards, standard checklists and acceptance criteria
- The quality criteria can be used to determine when the product is fit for purpose
- The types of quality inspection required are able to verify whether the product meets its stated quality criteria
- The Senior User(s) confirms that their requirements of the product, as defined in the Product Description, are accurately defined
- The Senior Supplier(s) confirms that the requirements of the product, as defined in the Product Description, can be achieved.

Identifier[50]	
Title[51]	

Purpose

(This defines the purpose that the product will fulfil and who will use it. Is it a means to an end or an end in itself? It is helpful in understanding the product's functions, size, quality, complexity, robustness etc.)

Composition

(This is a list of the parts of the product. For example, if the product were a report, this would be a list of the expected chapters or sections)

Derivation

(What are the source products from which this product is derived? Examples are: a design is derived from a specification; a product is bought in from a supplier; a statement of the expected benefits is obtained from the user; or a product is obtained from another department or team)

Format and Presentation

(The characteristics of the product - for example, if the product were a report, this would specify whether the report should be a document, presentation slides or an email)

Development Skills Required

(An indication of the skills required to develop the product or a pointer to which area(s) should supply the development resources. Identification of the actual people may be left until planning the stage in which the product is to be created

---

[50] Unique key, probably allocated by the configuration management method and likely to include the project name, item name and version number
[51] Name by which the product is known

Quality Criteria[52]	Quality Tolerance[53]	Quality Method[54]	Quality Skills Required[55]

Quality Responsibilities

Role	Responsible Individuals
Product Producer	
Product Reviewer(s)	
Product Approver(s)	

---

[52] To what quality specification must the product be produced, and what quality measurements will be applied by those inspecting the finished product? This might be a simple reference to one or more common standards that are documented elsewhere, or it might be a full explanation of some yardstick to be applied. If the product is to be developed and approved in different states (e.g. dismantled machinery, moved machinery and reassembled machinery), then the quality criteria should be grouped into those that apply for each state

[53] Details of any range in the quality criteria within which the product would be acceptable

[54] The kinds of quality method - for example, design verification, pilot, test, inspection or review - that are to be used to check the quality or functionality of the product

[55] An indication of the skills required to undertake the quality method or a pointer to which area(s) should supply the checking resources. Identification of the actual people may be left until planning the stage in which the quality inspection is to be done

PRINCE2™ - Product Status Account

Project Name:	
Date:	**Release:** Draft/Final
Author:	
Owner:	
Client:	
Document Number:	

Note: This document is only valid on the day it was printed

Revision History

Date of next revision:

Revision Date	Previous Revision Date	Summary of Changes	Changes Marked

Approvals

This document requires the following approvals. A signed copy should be placed in the project files.

Name	Signature	Title	Date of Issue	Version

Distribution

This document has been distributed to:

Name	Title	Date of Issue	Version

Overview

Purpose The Product Status Account provides information about the state of products within defined limits. The limits can vary. For example, the report could cover the entire project, a particular stage, a particular area of the project, or the history of a specific product. It is particularly useful if the Project Manager wishes to confirm the version number of products.

Contents The format following on page 3 is an example of the type of information the Project Manager may request as a Status Account on a Product or set of Products. Depending on the purpose of the request the Project Manager may request more or less information. This format would be repeated for each product included in the request.

Advice *The Product Status Account is derived from the Configuration Item Records and the Stage Plan.*

A Product Status Account can take a number of formats, including: Document, spreadsheet or report from a database; Output from a project management tool.

The following quality criteria should be observed:
- The details and dates match those in the Stage Plan
- The product name is consistent with the product breakdown structure and the name in the Configuration Item Record.

Product Status Account

Report Scope[56]	
Date Produced	
Product Status (repeated for each product included in the report scope)	
Product Identifier	
Product Title	
Version	
Status and date of status change	
Product State	
Owner	
Copy-holders	
Location	
User(s)	

Producer		Date Allocated	
Baseline Date planned		Actual	
Planned date of next baseline			
List of related items			
List of related Issues and risks[57]			

---

[56] Describing the scope of the report (e.g. for the entire project, by stage, by product type, by supplier etc. The product's attribute can be used to select the subset of products for the report)

[57] Including changes pending and approved

PRINCE2™ - Project Brief

Project Name:			
Date:		**Release:**	Draft/Final
Author:			
Owner:			
Client:			
Document Number:			

Note: This document is only valid on the day it was printed

Revision History

Date of next revision:

Revision Date	Previous Revision Date	Summary of Changes	Changes Marked

Approvals

This document requires the following approvals. A signed copy should be placed in the project files.

Name	Signature	Title	Date of Issue	Version

Distribution

This document has been distributed to:

Name	Title	Date of Issue	Version

Overview

Purpose A Project Brief is used to provide a full and firm foundation for the initiation of the project and is created in the Starting up a Project process.

In the Initiating a Project process, the contents of the Project Brief are extended and refined in the Project Initiation Documentation, after which the Project Brief is no longer maintained.

Contents *The Project Brief should cover the following topics.*

Project Definition
Outline Business Case
Project product Description
Project Approach
Project management team Structure
Role Descriptions
References

Advice *The Project Brief is derived from: A project mandate supplied at the start of the project; Programme management - if the project is part of a programme, the Project Brief is likely to be supplied by the programme, and therefore it will not have to be derived from a project mandate; Discussions with corporate management regarding corporate strategy and any policies and standards that apply; Discussions with the Project Board and users if the project mandate is incomplete or if no project mandate is provided; Discussions with the operations and maintenance organization (if applicable); Discussion with the (potential) suppliers regarding specialist development lifecycles that could be used; Lessons Log.*

A Project Brief can take a number of formats, including: Document or presentation slides; Entry in a project management tool.

The following quality criteria should be observed:

- It is brief because its purpose at this point is to provide a firm basis on which to initiate a project. It will later be refined and expanded as part of the Project Initiation Documentation
- The Project Brief accurately reflects the project mandate and the requirements of the business and the users
- The project approach considers a range of solutions, such as: bespoke or off-the-shelf; contracted out or developed in-house; designed from new or a modified existing product
- The project approach has been selected which maximizes the chance of achieving overall success for the project
- The project objectives, project approach and strategies are consistent with the organization's corporate social responsibility directive
- The project objectives are Specific, Measurable, Achievable, Realistic and Time-bound (SMART).

Project Definition
(Explaining what the project needs to achieve. It should include information on the sections given below)

Background

Project objectives
(covering time, cost, quality, scope, risk and benefit performance goals)

Desired outcomes

Project scope and exclusions

Constraints and assumptions

Project tolerances

The user(s) and any other known interested parties

Interfaces

Outline Business Case
(Reasons why the project is needed, and the business option selected. This will later be developed into a detailed Business Case during the Initiating a Project process)

Project Product Description
(Including the customer's quality expectations, user acceptance criteria, and operations and maintenance acceptance criteria)

Project Approach
(To define the choice of solution that will be used within the project to deliver the business option selected from the Business Case, taking into consideration the operational environment into which the solution must fit)

Project Management Team Structure
(A chart showing who will be involved with the project)

Role Descriptions
(For the project management team and any other key resources identified at this time)

References
(To any associated documents or products)

PRINCE2™ - Project Initiation Documentation

Project Name:			
Date:		**Release:**	Draft/Final
Author:			
Owner:			
Client:			
Document Number:			

Note: This document is only valid on the day it was printed

Revision History

Date of next revision:

Revision Date	Previous Revision Date	Summary of Changes	Changes Marked

Approvals

This document requires the following approvals. A signed copy should be placed in the project files.

Name	Signature	Title	Date of Issue	Version

Distribution

This document has been distributed to:

Name	Title	Date of Issue	Version

Overview

Purpose The purpose of the Project Initiation Documentation is to define the project, in order to form the basis for its management and an assessment of its overall success. The Project Initiation Documentation gives the direction and scope of the project and (along with the Stage Plan) forms the 'contract' between the Project Manager and the Project Board.

The three primary uses of the Project Initiation Documentation are to:

- Ensure that the project has a sound basis before asking the Project Board to make any major commitment to the project
- Act as a base document against which the Project Board and Project Manager can assess progress, issues and ongoing viability questions
- Provide a single source of reference about the project so that people joining the 'temporary organization' can quickly and easily find out what the project is about, and how it is being managed.

The Project Initiation Documentation is a living product in that it should always reflect the current status, plans and controls of the project. Its component products will need to be updated and re-baselined, as necessary, at the end of each stage, to reflect the current status of its constituent parts.

The version of the Project Initiation Documentation that was used to gain authorization for the project is preserved as the basis against which performance will later be assessed when closing the project.

Contents *The Project Initiation Documentation should cover the following topics.*

Project Definition
Project Approach
Business Case
Project Management Team Structure
Role Descriptions
Quality Management Approach
Change Control Approach
Risk Management Approach
Communication Management Approach
Project Plan
Project Controls
Tailoring of Prince2

Advice *The Project Initiation Documentation is derived from the Project Brief and discussions with user, business and supplier stakeholders for input on methods, standards and controls.*

The Project Initiation Documentation could be a single document; an index for a collection of documents; a document with cross references to a number of other documents; a collection of information in a project management tool.

The following quality criteria should be observed:

- *The Project Initiation Documentation correctly represents the project*
- *It shows a viable, achievable project that is in line with corporate strategy or overall programme needs*
- *The project management team structure is complete, with names and titles. All the roles have been considered and are backed up by agreed role descriptions. The relationships and lines of authority are clear. If necessary, the project management team structure says to whom the Project Board reports*
- *It clearly shows a control, reporting and direction regime that can be implemented, appropriate to the scale, risk and importance of the project to corporate or programme management*

- The controls cover the needs of the Project Board, Project Manager and Team Managers and satisfy any delegated assurance requirements
- It is clear who will administer each control
- The project objectives, approach and strategies are consistent with the organization's corporate social responsibility directive, and the project controls are adequate to ensure that the project remains compliant with such a directive
- Consideration has been given to the format of the Project Initiation Documentation. For small projects a single document is appropriate. For large projects it is more appropriate for the Project Initiation Documentation to be a collection of stand-alone documents. The volatility of each element of the Project Initiation Documentation should be used to assess whether it should be stand-alone, e.g. elements that are likely to change frequently are best separated out.

Project Definition
(Explaining what the project needs to achieve. It should include information on the sections given below)

Background

Project objectives
(covering time, cost, quality, scope, risk and benefit performance goals)

Desired outcomes

Project scope and exclusions

Constraints and assumptions

The user(s) and any other known interested parties

Interfaces

Project Approach
(To define the choice of solution that will be used in the project to deliver the business option selected from the Business Case, taking into consideration the operational environment into which the solution must fit)

Business Case
(Describing the justification for the project based on estimated costs, risks and benefits)

Project Management Team Structure
(A chart showing who will be involved with the project)

Role Descriptions
(For the project management team and any other key resources)

Quality Management Approach
(Describing the quality techniques and standards to be applied, and the responsibilities for achieving the required quality levels)

Change Control Approach
(Describing how and by whom the project's products will be controlled and protected)

Risk Management Approach
(Describing the specific risk management techniques and standards to be applied, and the responsibilities for achieving an effective risk management procedure)

Communication Management Approach
(To define the parties interested in the project and the means and frequency of communication between them and the project)

Project Plan
(Describing how and when the project's objectives are to be achieved, by showing the major products, activities and resources required on the project. It provides a baseline against which to monitor the project's progress stage by stage)

Project Controls
(Summarizing the project-level controls such as stage boundaries, agreed tolerances, monitoring and reporting)

Tailoring of PRINCE2
(A summary of how PRINCE2 will be tailored for the project.)

PRINCE2™ - Project Product Description

Project Name:			
Date:		**Release:**	Draft/Final
Author:			
Owner:			
Client:			
Document Number:			

Note: This document is only valid on the day it was printed

Revision History

Date of next revision:

Revision Date	Previous Revision Date	Summary of Changes	Changes Marked

Approvals

This document requires the following approvals. A signed copy should be placed in the project files.

Name	Signature	Title	Date of Issue	Version

Distribution

This document has been distributed to:

Name	Title	Date of Issue	Version

Overview

Purpose The Project Product Description is a special form of Product Description that defines what the project must deliver in order to gain acceptance. It is used to:

- Gain agreement from the user on the project's scope and requirements
- Define the customer's quality expectations
- Define the acceptance criteria, method and responsibilities for the project.

The Product Description for the project product is created in the Starting up a Project process as part of the initial scoping activity, and is refined during the Initiating a Project process when creating the Project Plan. It is subject to formal change control and should be checked at stage boundaries (during Managing a Stage Boundary) to see if any changes are required. It is used by the Closing a Project process as part of the verification that the project has delivered what was expected of it, and that the acceptance criteria have been met.

Contents The Project Product Description should cover the following topics.

Title
Purpose
Composition
Derivation
Development Skills Required
Customers Quality Expectations
Acceptance Criteria
Project Level Quality Tolerances
Acceptance Method
Acceptance Responsibilities

Advice The Project Product Description is derived from the project mandate, discussions with the Senior User and Executive – possibly via scoping workshops and the request for proposal (if in a commercial customer/supplier environment).

A Product Description for the project product can take a number of formats, including: Document, presentation slides or mind map; or Entry in a project management tool.

The following quality criteria should be observed:

- The purpose is clear
- The composition defines the complete scope of the project
- The acceptance criteria form the complete list against which the project will be assessed
- The acceptance criteria address the requirements of all the key stakeholders (e.g. operations and maintenance)
- The Project Product Description defines how the users and the operational and maintenance organizations will assess the acceptability of the finished product(s):
    - All criteria are measurable
    - Each criterion is individually realistic
    - The criteria are realistic and consistent as a set. For example, high quality, early delivery and low cost may not go together
    - All criteria can be proven within the project life (e.g. the maximum

throughput of a water pump), or by proxy measures that provide reasonable indicators as to whether acceptance criteria will be achieved post-project (e.g. a water pump that complies with design and manufacturing standards of reliability)
- The quality expectations have considered:
  - The characteristics of the key quality requirements (e.g. fast/slow, large/small, national/global)
  - The elements of the customer's quality management system that should be used
  - Any other standards that should be used
  - The level of customer/staff satisfaction that should be achieved if surveyed.

Title
(Name by which the project is known)

Purpose
(This defines the purpose that the project's product will fulfil and who will use it. It is helpful in understanding the product's functions, size, quality, complexity, robustness etc.)

Composition
(Description of the major products to be delivered by the project)

Derivation
(What are the source products from which this product is derived? Examples are: Existing products to be modified; design specifications; a feasibility report or project mandate)

Development Skills Required
(An indication of the skills required to develop the product, or a pointer to which area(s) should supply the development resources)

Customer's Quality Expectations
(A description of the quality expected of the project's product and the standards and processes that will need to be applied to achieve that quality. They will impact on every part of the product development, and thus on time and cost. The quality expectations are captured in discussions with the customer. Where possible, expectations should be prioritized)

Acceptance Criteria[58]	Project Level Quality Tolerances[59]	Acceptance Method[60]	Acceptance Responsibilities[61]

---

[58] A prioritized list of criteria that the project's product must meet before the customer will accept it - i.e. measurable definitions of the attributes that must apply to the set of products to be acceptable to key stakeholders (and, in particular, the users and the operational and maintenance organizations). Examples are: ease of use, ease of support, ease of maintenance, appearance, major functions, development costs, running costs, capacity, availability, reliability, security, accuracy or performance

[59] Specifying any tolerances that may apply for the acceptance criteria

---

[60] Stating the means by which acceptance will be confirmed. This may simply be a case of confirming that all the project's products have been approved or may involve describing complex handover arrangements for the project's product, including any phased handover of the project's products
[61] Defining who will be responsible for confirming acceptance

PRINCE2™ - Quality Management Approach

Project Name:			
Date:		**Release:**	Draft/Final
Author:			
Owner:			
Client:			
Document Number:			

Note: This document is only valid on the day it was printed

Revision History

Date of next revision:

Revision Date	Previous Revision Date	Summary of Changes	Changes Marked

Approvals

This document requires the following approvals. A signed copy should be placed in the project files.

Name	Signature	Title	Date of Issue	Version

Distribution

This document has been distributed to:

Name	Title	Date of Issue	Version

Overview

Purpose   A Quality Management Approach is used to define the quality techniques and standards to be applied, and the various responsibilities for achieving the required quality levels, during the project.

Contents   The Quality Management Approach should cover the following topics.

Introduction
Quality Management Procedure
Tools & techniques
Records
Reporting
Timing of Quality Management Activities
Roles & Responsibilities

Advice   *The Quality Management Approach is derived from the: Project Board; Project Brief, Project management team structure (for roles and responsibilities), Project Product Description (for the customer's quality expectations and acceptance criteria); Organizational standards; Supplier and customer quality management systems; Configuration management requirements; Change control requirements; Corporate or programme strategies; Facilitated workshops and informal discussions.*

A Quality Management Approach can take a number of formats, including: Stand-alone document or a section in the Project Initiation Document; Entry in a project management tool.

The following quality criteria should be observed:

- The strategy clearly defines ways in which the customer's quality expectations will be met
- The defined ways are sufficient to achieve the required quality
- Responsibilities for quality are defined up to a level that is independent of the project and Project Manager
- The strategy conforms to the supplier's and customer's quality management systems
- The strategy conforms to the corporate or programme quality policy
- The approaches to assuring quality for the project are appropriate in the light of the standards selected.

Introduction
(States the purpose, objectives and scope, and identifies who is responsible for the strategy)

Quality Management Procedure
(A description of (or reference to) the quality management procedure to be used. Any variance from corporate or programme management quality standards should be highlighted, together with a justification for the variance)

The Procedure should cover the following topics:

Quality planning

Quality control
(The project's approach to quality control activities. This may include: Quality standards, Templates and forms to be employed (e.g. Product Description(s), Quality Register), Definitions of types of quality methods (e.g. inspection, pilot), and Metrics to be employed in support of quality control)

Quality assurance
(The project's approach to quality assurance activities. This may include: Responsibilities of the Project Board, Compliance audits, and Corporate or programme management reviews)

Tools and Techniques
(Refers to any quality management systems or tools to be used, and any preference for techniques which may be used for each step in the quality management procedure)

Records
(Definition of what quality records will be required and where they will be stored including the composition and format of the Quality Register)

Reporting
(Describes any quality management reports that are to be produced, their purpose, timing and recipients)

Timing of Quality Management Activities
(States when formal quality management activities are to be undertaken, for example audits (this may be a reference to the Quality Register))

Roles and Responsibilities
(Defines the roles and responsibilities for quality management activities, including those with quality responsibilities from corporate or programme management)

PRINCE2™ - Risk Management Approach

Project Name:			
Date:		**Release:**	Draft/Final
Author:			
Owner:			
Client:			
Document Number:			

Note: This document is only valid on the day it was printed

Revision History

Date of next revision:

Revision Date	Previous Revision Date	Summary of Changes	Changes Marked

Approvals

This document requires the following approvals. A signed copy should be placed in the project files.

Name	Signature	Title	Date of Issue	Version

Distribution

This document has been distributed to:

Name	Title	Date of Issue	Version

Overview

Purpose A Risk Management Approach describes the specific risk management techniques and standards to be applied and the responsibilities for achieving an effective risk management procedure.

Contents The Risk Management Approach should cover the following topics.

Introduction
Risks Management Procedure
Tools & Techniques
Records
Reporting
Timings of Risk Management Activities
Roles & Responsibilities
Scales
Proximity
Risk Categories
Risk Response Categories
Early Warning Indicators
Risk Tolerance
Risk Budget

Advice The Risk Management Approach is derived from the: Project Brief; Business Case; The corporate or programme management's risk management guide, strategy or policy.

A Risk Management Approach can take a number of formats, including: Stand-alone document or a section in the Project Initiation Document; Entry in a project management tool.

The following quality criteria should be observed:
- Responsibilities are clear and understood by both customer and supplier
- The risk management procedure is clearly documented and can be understood by all parties
- Scales, expected value and proximity definitions are clear and unambiguous
- The chosen scales are appropriate for the level of control required
- Risk reporting requirements are fully defined.

Introduction
(States the purpose, objectives and scope, and identifies who is responsible for the strategy)

Risk Management Procedure
(A description of (or reference to) the risk management procedure to be used. Any variance from corporate or programme management standards should be highlighted, together with a justification for the variance.)

The procedure should cover activities such as:

Identify

Assess

Plan

Implement

Communicate

Tools and Techniques
(Refers to any risk management systems or tools to be used, and any preference for techniques which may be used for each step in the risk management procedure)

Records
(Definition of the composition and format of the Risk Register and any other risk records to be used by the project)

Reporting
(Describes any risk management reports that are to be produced, including their purpose, timing and recipients)

Timing of Risk Management Activities
(States when formal risk management activities are to be undertaken - for example, at end stage assessments)

Roles and Responsibilities
(Defines the roles and responsibilities for risk management activities)

Scales
(Defines the scales for estimating probability and impact for the project to ensure that the scales for cost and time (for instance) are relevant to the cost and timeframe of the project. These may be shown in the form of probability impact grids giving the criteria for each level within the scale, e.g. for 'very high', 'high', 'medium', 'low' and 'very low')

Proximity
(Guidance on how proximity for risk events is to be assessed. Proximity reflects the fact that risks will occur at particular times and the severity of their impact will vary according to when they occur. Typical proximity categories will be: imminent, within the stage, within the project, beyond the project)

Risk Categories
(Definition of the risk categories to be used (if at all). These may be derived from a risk breakdown structure or prompt list. If no risks have been recorded against a category, this may suggest that the risk identification has not been as thorough as it should have been)

Risk Response Categories
(Definition of the risk response categories to be used, which themselves depend on whether a risk is a perceived threat or an opportunity)

Early-warning Indicators
(Definition of any indicators to be used to track critical aspects of the project so that if certain predefined levels are reached, corrective action will be triggered. They will be selected for their relevance to the project objectives)

Risk Tolerance
(Defining the threshold levels of risk exposure, which, when exceeded, require the risk to be escalated to the next level of management. (For example, a project-level risk tolerance could be set as any risk that, should it occur, would result in loss of trading. Such risks would need to be escalated to corporate or programme management.) The risk tolerance should define the risk expectations of corporate or programme management and the Project Board)

Risk Budget
(Describing whether a risk budget is to be established and, if so, how it will be used)

PRINCE2™ - Work Package

Project Name:			
Date:		**Release:**	Draft/Final
Author:			
Owner:			
Client:			
Document Number:			

Note: This document is only valid on the day it was printed

Revision History

Date of next revision:

Revision Date	Previous Revision Date	Summary of Changes	Changes Marked

Approvals

This document requires the following approvals. A signed copy should be placed in the project files.

Name	Signature	Title	Date of Issue	Version

Distribution

This document has been distributed to:

Name	Title	Date of Issue	Version

Overview

Purpose A Work Package is a set of information about one or more required products collated by the Project Manager to pass responsibility for work or delivery formally to a Team Manager or team member.

Contents A Work Package should cover the following topics. The content may vary greatly according to the relationship between the Project Manager and the recipient of the Work Package.

> Work package Authorisation
> Description
> Techniques, Processes, Procedures
> Development Interfaces
> Operations & Maintenance Interfaces
> Change Control Requirements
> Joint Agreements
> Tolerances
> Constraints
> Reporting, Handling & Escalation
> Extracts or References
> Approval Method
> Work Package Acceptance

Advice A Work Package is derived from any existing commercial agreements between the customer and supplier (if appropriate); Quality Management Approach; Change Control Approach; Stage Plan

> A Work Package can take a number of formats, including: Document; Oral conversation between the Project Manager and a Team Manager; Entry in a project management tool.
>
> The Work Package will vary in content and in degree of formality, depending on circumstances.
>
> Where the work is being conducted by a team working directly under the Project Manager, the Work Package may be an oral instruction - although there are good reasons for putting it in writing, such as avoidance of misunderstanding and providing a link to performance assessment. Where the work is being carried out by a supplier under a contract and the Project Manager is part of the customer organization, there is a need for a formal written instruction in line with standards laid down in that contract.
>
> The following quality criteria should be observed:
> - The required Work Package is clearly defined and understood by the assigned resource
> - There is a Product Description for each required product, with clearly identified and acceptable quality criteria
> - The Product Description(s) matches up with the other Work Package documentation
> - Standards for the work are agreed
> - The defined standards are in line with those applied to similar products
> - All necessary interfaces have been defined
> - The reporting arrangements include the provision for raising issues and risks
> - There is agreement between the Project Manager and the recipient on exactly what is to be done
> - There is agreement on the constraints, including effort, cost and targets

- *The dates and effort are in line with those shown in the Stage Plan for the current management stage*
- *Reporting arrangements are defined*
- *Any requirement for independent attendance at, and participation in, quality activities is defined.*

Work Package Authorisation

Title	
Person Authorised[62]	
Date[63]	

Description
(A description of the work to be done)

Techniques, Processes and Procedures
(Any techniques, tools, standards, processes or procedures to be used in the creation of the specialist products)

Development Interfaces
(Interfaces that must be maintained while developing the products. These may be people providing information or those who need to receive information)

Operations and Maintenance Interfaces
(Identification of any specialist products with which the product(s) in the Work Package will have to interface during their operational life. These may be other products to be produced by the project, existing products, or those to be produced by other projects (for example, if the project is part of a programme)

Change Control Requirements
(A statement of any arrangements that must be made by the producer for: version control of the products in the Work Package; obtaining copies of other products or their Product Descriptions; submission of the product to configuration management; any storage or security requirements; and who, if anyone, needs to be advised of changes in the status of the Work Package)

---

[62] The name of the Team Manager or individual with whom the agreement has been made
[63] The date of the agreement between the Project Manager and the Team Manager/person authorised

Joint Agreements
(Details of the agreements on effort, cost, start and end dates, and key milestones for the Work Package)

Tolerances
(Details of the tolerances for the Work Package (the tolerances will be for time and cost but may also include scope and risk))

Constraints
(Any constraints (apart from the tolerances) on the work, people to be involved, timings, charges, rules to be followed (for example, security and safety) etc.)

Reporting Arrangements
(The expected frequency and content of Checkpoint Reports)

Problem Handling and Escalation
(This refers to the procedure for raising issues and risks)

Extracts or References
(Any extracts or references to related documents, specifically:
- Stage Plan extract This will be the relevant section of the Stage Plan for the current management stage or will be a pointer to it
- Product Description(s) This would normally be an attachment of the Product Description(s) for the products identified in the Work Package (note that the Product Description contains the quality methods to be used)

Approval method
(The person, role or group who will approve the completed products within the Work Package, and how the Project Manager is to be advised of completion of the products and Work Package)

Work Package Acceptance	
Person Accepting[64]	
Date[65]	
Assessment and feedback[66]	

---

[64] The Project Manager or other person accepting the work package on the Project Manager's behalf
[65] The date of acceptance
[66] This can be used by the person accepting the work package to provide comments on the work package possibly to go towards performance appraisal for the individual or teams involved

Conclusion

As promised at the beginning of this book, the email address is Carl@pmguide.co.uk and mention the book and I will send you electronic versions of the templates and include some new PowerPoint and Excel templates

Thank you looking at the book and hopefully if the book was useful, you would like to write a review

Thank you and good luck with your Project,

Carl

www.ingramcontent.com/pod-product-compliance
Lightning Source LLC
Chambersburg PA
CBHW050325230526
45471CB00005B/2359